CRAZY TO BE ALIVE
IN SUCH A
STRANGE WORLD

CRAZY TO BE ALIVE IN SUCH A STRANGE WORLD

POEMS ABOUT PEOPLE

Selected by NANCY LARRICK

Photographs by Alexander L. Crosby

M. EVANS AND CO., INC. / New York, N.Y. 10017

M. Evans and Company titles are distributed in
the United States by the J. B. Lippincott Company,
East Washington Square, Philadelphia, Pa. 19105;
and in Canada by McClelland & Stewart Ltd.,
25 Hollinger Road, Toronto M4B 3G2, Ontario

LIBRARY OF CONGRESS CATALOGING IN PUBLICATION DATA
Main entry under title:

Crazy to be alive in such a strange world.

Includes index.
SUMMARY: A collection of poems by American authors
portraying old people, married people, lonely people,
black people, and others.
 1. Children's poetry, American. [1. American
poetry—20th century—Collections] I. Larrick, Nancy.
PN6110.C4C79   811'.5'08   76-49667
ISBN 0-87131-225-5

Design by Joel Schick

Manufactured in the United States of America

9 8 7 6 5 4 3 2 1

Thanks are due to the following authors, publishers, publications, and agents for
permission to use the material included.
    SAMUEL W. ALLEN for "To Satch." Reprinted by permission of the author.
    ATHENEUM PUBLISHERS, INC. for "74th Street" from The Malibu and Other
Poems by Myra Cohn Livingston (A Margaret K. McElderry Book). Copyright © 1972
by Myra Cohn Livingston. Used by permission of Atheneum Publishers. Also for "Old
People" from The Way Things Are and Other Poems by Myra Cohn Livingston (A
Margaret K. McElderry Book). Copyright © 1974 by Myra Cohn Livingston. Used by
permission of Atheneum Publishers. Also for "Vermont Conversation" from The Apple
Vendor's Fair by Patricia Hubbell. Copyright © 1963 by Patricia Hubbell. Used by
permission of Atheneum Publishers. Also for "The Umbilical" from Finding a Poem by
Eve Merriam. Copyright © 1970 by Eve Merriam. Used by permission of Atheneum
Publishers.

LITTLE, BROWN AND COMPANY for "The Portrait" from *The Testing Tree: Poems* by Stanley Kunitz. Copyright © 1971 by Stanley Kunitz. Reprinted by permission of Little, Brown and Company in association with the Atlantic Monthly Press.

JOHN LOGAN for "The Picnic" from *Ghosts of the Heart*. Copyright © 1960 by University of Chicago Press. Reprinted by permission of John Logan.

MACMILLAN PUBLISHING CO., INC. for "A Winter Scene" from *The Self-Made Man* by Reed Whittemore. © 1958 by Reed Whittemore. Originally published in *Poetry*. Reprinted by permission of Macmillan Publishing Co., Inc.

ELLEN C. MASTERS for "Cooney Potter" from *Spoon River Anthology* by Edgar Lee Masters, published by Macmillan Publishing Company, Inc. Reprinted by permission of Ellen C. Masters.

WILLIAM C. MATCHETT for "Aunt Alice in April" from *Water Ouzel and Other Poems* (Houghton Mifflin). Copyright © 1955 by William H. Matchett. Reprinted by permission of William H. Matchett.

WILLIAM MORROW & CO., INC. for "Conversations," "Legacies," and "Mothers" from *My House* by Nikki Giovanni. Copyright © 1972 by Nikki Giovanni. Reprinted by permission of William Morrow & Co., Inc.

LISA MUELLER for "Civilizing the Child." Originally appeared in *Poetry*. Reprinted by permission of the author.

NEW DIRECTIONS PUBLISHING CORPORATION for "The pennycandystore beyond the El" from *A Coney Island of the Mind* by Lawrence Ferlinghetti. Copyright © 1958 by Lawrence Ferlinghetti. Reprinted by permission of New Directions Publishing Corporation. Also for "The Rainwalkers" from *The Jacob's Ladder* by Denise Levertov. Copyright © 1961 by Denise Levertov Goodman. Reprinted by permission of New Directions Publishing Corporation. Also for "An Easy Decision" from *Collected Poems (When We Were Here Together)* by Kenneth Patchen. Copyright © 1957 by New Directions Publishing Corporation. Reprinted by permission of New Directions Publishing Corporation. Also for "Simple Soul" (from "Depression" ii), "Puerto Ricans in New York, I," "Puerto Ricans in New York, II," and "The young fellow walks about" from *By the Waters of Manhattan* by Charles Reznikoff. Copyright 1936, 1941, © 1959 by Charles Reznikoff. Reprinted by permission of New Directions Publishing Corporation. Also for "The Paper Lantern" (from "Recuerdo" iii) from *In the Winter of Cities* by Tennessee Williams. Copyright © 1956 by Tennessee Williams. Reprinted by permission of New Directions Publishing Corporation. Also for "The Return to Work" from *Collected Earlier Poems* by William Carlos Williams. Copyright 1939, 1951 by William Carlos Williams. First published in *The New Yorker*. Reprinted by permission of New Directions Publishing Corporation.

THE NEW YORKER for "To Kate Skating Better Than Her Date" by David Daiches (reprinted by permission; © 1957 by The New Yorker Magazine, Inc.), and "How Tuesday Began" by Kathleen Fraser (reprinted by permission; © 1963 The New Yorker Magazine, Inc.), from *The New Yorker Book of Poems*.

OCTOBER HOUSE for "Those Winter Sundays" from *Selected Poems* by Robert Hayden. Copyright © 1966 by Robert Hayden. Reprinted by permission of October House.

MANNA LOWENFELS PERPELITT for "Speaking: The Hero" by Felix Pollak from *Where Is Vietnam? American Poets Respond*, edited by Walter Lowenfels.

*In memory of my father
Herbert S. Larrick
who led me to appreciate
the diversity and the beauty
of human nature.*

CONTENTS

CRAZY
TO BE
ALIVE

This book began many years ago when I was growing up in Winchester, Virginia. I wasn't collecting poetry then, but I know now that I was collecting people—the shy ones and the headstrong, the crusty and the jubilant, who made up the great diversity of that small southern town.

In those days the children had the run of the town, ranging on their roller skates or bikes from one end to the other and often into the country. Deep roots in that community had held families there for generations, so parents, grandparents, and even great-grandparents knew one another well. As a matter of course, they welcomed the new generation into their homes for dinner and "spending the night" as we called it.

My Brownie No. 2 camera didn't produce any lasting snap-shots, but in my memory there are countless portraits of those amazing people who by this time make a living documentary for me. One of the grandfathers—not my own—was extremely deaf and carried an ear trumpet which he would lift from around his neck, adjusting one end to his ear and holding the other for you to speak into. I remember him leaning over so some youngster could reach the mouthpiece and extend the morning's greetings. No child's comment was too trivial for him to reply to with the utmost graciousness.

Now I marvel at that extraordinary courtesy toward children, but it was the accepted way in my childhood. I recall a friend whom my father would frequently bring home for dinner— always a hearty eater and a great talker, who invariably bowed as he shook my hand and addressed me as "Miss Nancy" even when I was only eight or ten. He used the same formality with my mother and presumably felt her little girl deserved no less.

On one occasion Mother served cupcakes in little frilled paper cups. On the second round my father pointed out that Mr. Chiles had eaten the cup along with the cake, but the dignified bearing never faltered.

At that time the Civil War was very much a part of the community because many could give firsthand reports. I heard the story of the burning of Richmond from one who, as a slave, had fled with her family to safety. My grandmother was a teenager during "the war," as it was always referred to, and gave me the autograph album in which Confederate soldiers recorded tender verses to "Dear Jennie" on their way to or from battle in the Shenandoah Valley. It seemed only natural to find that some of those young soldiers had become the grandparents of my schoolmates in that same town.

Two of my young friends lived across the street from the county jail presided over by Boss Pannett, the sheriff, and his wife, who always had fresh cakes and cookies for neighborhood children. In later years, one of the mothers noted that her boys grew up thinking the jail was the place you could go for an afternoon treat if you had been very good all morning.

One of my most vivid recollections centers around a gentle old man who had repaired the steps of our kitchen porch. Some months later he came with a petition to save his grandson from the electric chair. Would my parents be willing to sign? The town had been torn apart by the case of the young teenager who had shot and killed a solid citizen on his front porch. The old man quietly apologized for his grandson: "He is only a boy, you know." I relayed the message to my father, a lawyer, fully expecting him to be as eager for the death sentence as other adults I had heard discussing the case. "Of course I'll sign," he said at once. "Who am I to deprive someone of his life?" My position on capital punishment was formed then and there.

The public library in our town was a treasure house for us as children. As we clattered up the narrow circular iron stairway to the children's collection, there would invariably be a resounding "Shush" from the librarians whom we felt to be unnecessarily severe. When we exhausted the supply of children's books and tried to push into the adult section, both eyebrows and barriers were raised. To my mother I explained that my friend Judy McGuire was already reading detective stories, which somehow seemed more advanced, indeed more wicked, than they do now. Mother pressed for an exact title and acquiesced completely when Judy cited *Anne of Green Gables* as "a thrilling detective story." The fact that Judy pronounced "Gables" as though it rhymed with "babbles" only dawned on me years later.

Just as these living portraits are coming into focus for me, so are the poetic portraits I was meeting at the same time. These are the poems I seem to remember best, perhaps because the living portrait collection was becoming part of me.

In high school I met "My Last Duchess," Browning's poem written in 1842. Our English teacher read with such feeling that I seem to remember every word as he stood, yardstick in hand, pointing to the marked-up blackboard reciting: "That's my last Duchess, painted on the wall,/ Looking as if she were alive." We were transported.

It was not until I was in college and reading Chaucer that I also met the world of A.A. Milne and Christopher Robin. When the Dean, a distinguished historian, learned that I had never heard of James James Morrison Morrison and Emmilene, she gave me a copy of *When We Were Very Young*. "You need to know these people," she said earnestly. And of course she was right.

Spoon River Anthology by Edgar Lee Masters hit me after I began teaching in the same small town where I had grown up. Then I learned that my students were equally fascinated by what they sometimes called "people poems," and *Spoon River* is a veritable portrait gallery.

Virtually every poet has fixed a penetrating eye on some individual in his or her life and then given us a poetic portrait that is unforgettable. What a picture these poems give of our world and of ourselves! Vivid. Complex. Teeming. Like the old kaleidoscope which showed constant change in patterns of brilliant colors—none alike, none completely comprehensible or predictable, and thus all the more fascinating!

Inevitably the people of poetry have become a part of me. I see them shoving into the subway or jogging down a country road. I remember a child's shy glance or hear a teenage shriek of delight. And as they come back to me again and again, I rejoice in being alive in this beautiful conglomeration of people.

Nancy Larrick

CRAZY TO BE ALIVE
IN SUCH A
STRANGE WORLD

ON
THE
STREET
WE
TWO
PASS

COMMITMENT IN A CITY

On the street we two pass.
I do not know you.
I did not see
if you are—
fat/thin,
dark/fair,
young/old.

If we should pass again
within the hour,
I would not know it.
Yet—
I am committed to
love you.

You are part of my city,
my universe, my being.
If you were not here
to pass me by,
a piece would be missing
from my jigsaw-puzzle day.

MARGARET TSUDA

The young fellow walks about
with nothing to do: he has lost his job.
"If I ever get another, I'll be hard!
You've got to be hard
to get on. I'll be hard, all right,"
he says bitterly. Takes out his cigarettes.
Only four or five left.
Looks at me out of the corner of his eye—
a stranger he has just met; hesitates;
and offers me a cigarette.

CHARLES REZNIKOFF

AN EASY DECISION

I had finished my dinner
Gone for a walk
It was fine
Out and I started whistling

It wasn't long before

I met a
Man and his wife riding on
A pony with seven
Kids running along beside them

I said hello and

Went on
Pretty soon I met another
Couple
This time with nineteen
Kids and all of them
Riding on
A big smiling hippopotamus

I invited them home

KENNETH PATCHEN

crazy
        to be alive in such a strange
                                world
with the band playing schmaltz
                in the classic bandshell
                                and the people
        on the benches under the clipped trees
                                and girls
    on the grass
                and the breeze blowing and the streamers
streaming
        and a fat man with a graflex
        and a dark woman with a dark dog she called
                                        Lucia
        and a cat on a leash
        and a pekinese with a blond baby
        and a cuban with a fedora
        and a bunch of boys posing for a group
                                picture
and just then
                while the band went right on playing
                                        schmaltz
a midget ran past shouting and waving his hat
                                at someone
        and a young man with a gay campaignbutton
came up and said
                Are you by any chance a registered
                        DEMOCRAT?

LAWRENCE FERLINGHETTI

HEY,
THIS
LITTLE KID
GETS
ROLLER
SKATES

74th STREET

Hey, this little kid gets roller skates.
She puts them on.
She stands up and almost
flops over backwards.
She sticks out a foot like
she's going somewhere and
falls down and
smacks her hand. She
grabs hold of a step to get up and
sticks out the other foot and
slides about six inches and
falls and
skins her knee.

And then, you know what?

She brushes off the dirt and the
blood and puts some
spit on it and then
sticks out the other foot

again.

MYRA COHN LIVINGSTON

LAUGHING CHILD

The child is on my shoulders.
In the prairie moonlight the child's legs
    hang over my shoulders.
She sits on my neck and I hear her calling
    me a good horse.
She slides down—and into the moon silver of
    a prairie stream.
She throws a stone and laughs at the clug-clug.

CARL SANDBURG

ROMPING

Silly. All giggles and ringlets and never
about to stop anything without fussing:
get down I say! Do you think I took your mother
to beget me a chimp for my shoulder?
I'm forty, boy, and no weight lifter.
Go find some energy your own size.
Get down!—Well, just once more.
There. Now get down, you baby-fat incubus.
Go ride your imagination. No, I don't care
how many kisses you will write a check for.
A million? Some banker you are. Still—
a million of anything is a lot of something.
All right. Once more, then. But just once. You hear?

JOHN CIARDI

SOIL SEARCHER

He stoops down, and crawls on hands and knees,
Stops, grabs a handful of dirt,
And bats it a few inches in the air,
Watching the dust fly up and down.

He sifts the same dirt again and again,
As if he didn't quite understand,
As if the flying particles should speak
To reveal to him some great secret.

He crawls to another spot, stops,
Waves his hand in front of his eyes
As if to free the spot to speak
And sifts the dirt again and again.

He's ten years old, but doesn't play
With other children—they leave him be.
His step's unsure, tentative, testing,
Guided by wide eyes that never seem to see.

J. JOYCE

HECTOR THE COLLECTOR

Hector the Collector
Collected bits of string,
Collected dolls with broken heads
And rusty bells that would not ring.
Pieces out of picture puzzles,
Bent-up nails and ice-cream sticks,
Twists of wires, worn-out tires,
Paper bags and broken bricks.
Old chipped vases, half shoelaces,
Gatlin' guns that wouldn't shoot,
Leaky boats that wouldn't float
And stopped-up horns that wouldn't toot.
Butter knives that had no handles,
Copper keys that fit no locks,
Rings that were too small for fingers,
Dried-up leaves and patched-up socks.
Worn-out belts that had no buckles,
'Lectric trains that had no tracks,
Airplane models, broken bottles,
Three-legged chairs and cups with cracks.
Hector the Collector
Loved these things with all his soul—
Loved them more than shining diamonds,
Loved them more than glistenin' gold.
Hector called to all the people,
"Come and share my treasure trunk!"
And all the silly sightless people
Came and looked . . . and called it junk.

SHEL SILVERSTEIN

JIMMY JET AND HIS TV SET

I'll tell you the story of Jimmy Jet—
And you know what I tell you is true.
He loved to watch his TV set
Almost as much as you.

He watched all day, he watched all night
Till he grew pale and lean,
From "The Early Show" to "The Late Late Show"
And all the shows between.

He watched till his eyes were frozen wide,
And his bottom grew into his chair.
And his chin turned into a tuning dial,
And antennae grew out of his hair.

And his brains turned into TV tubes,
And his face to a TV screen.
And two knobs saying "VERT." and "HORIZ."
Grew where his ears had been.

And he grew a plug that looked like a tail
So we plugged in little Jim.
And now instead of him watching TV
We all sit around watching him.

SHEL SILVERSTEIN

CAROL TOOK HER CLOTHES OFF

Carol took her clothes off
in the 6th grade
in the school yard
and maybe 20 of us
made a circle around her
so the teachers couldn't see
and one girl said
CAROL YOU'RE CRAZY
and Richard
he failed twice
felt her tit
and Carol bent her elbows like a chicken
and said she felt
uncaged and the girls giggled
but the boys didn't move
until the bell rang
and Carol ran back to class
her underwear
lying on the pavement.

BILL MESSENGER

UMBILICAL

You can take away my mother,
you can take away my sister,
but don't take away
my little transistor.

I can do without sunshine,
I can do without Spring,
but I can't do without
my ear to that thing.

I can live without water,
in a hole in the ground,
but I can't live without
that sound that sound that sound that sOWnd.

EVE MERRIAM

FOR SALE

One sister for sale!
One sister for sale!
One crying and spying young sister for sale!
I'm really not kidding,
So who'll start the bidding?
Do I hear a dollar?
A nickel?
A penny?
Oh, isn't there, isn't there, isn't there any
One kid who will buy this old sister for sale.
This crying and spying young sister for sale?

SHEL SILVERSTEIN

THE PAPER LANTERN
from *Recuerdo*

My sister was quicker at everything than I.

At five she could say the multiplication tables
    with barely a pause for breath,
    while I was employed
with frames of colored beads in Kindy Garden.

At eight she could play
              Idillio and The Scarf Dance
while I was chopping at scales and exercises.

At fifteen my sister
            no longer waited for me,
impatiently at the White Star Pharmacy corner
    but plunged headlong
    into the discovery, Love!

Then vanished completely—

for love's explosion, defined as early madness,
consumingly shone in her transparent heart for a season
and burned it out, a tissue-paper lantern!

    —torn from a string!
    —tumbled across a pavilion!

flickering three times, almost seeming to cry . . .
My sister was quicker at everything than I.

TENNESSEE WILLIAMS

FOREIGN STUDENT

In September she appeared
  row three, seat seven,
  heavy pleated skirt,
  plastic purse, tidy notepad,
there she sat,
silent,
straight from Tai Pei,
and she bowed
when I entered the room.
A model student
I noticed,
  though she walked
  alone through the halls,
every assignment neat,
on time, complete,
and she'd listen
when I talked.

But now it's May
and Si Lan
is called Lani.
She strides in
with Noriyo and Lynne
and Natavidad.
She wears slacks.
Her gear is crammed
into a macramé
shoulder sack.
And she chatters with Pete
during class
and
I'm glad.

BARBARA B. ROBINSON

MERRY-GO-ROUND
Colored child at carnival:

Where is the Jim Crow section
on this merry-go-round,
Mister, cause I want to ride?
Down South where I come from
White and colored
Can't sit side by side.
Down South on the train
There's a Jim Crow car.
On the bus we're put in the back—
But there ain't no back
To a merry-go-round!
Where's the horse
For a kid that's black?

LANGSTON HUGHES

INCIDENT

Once riding in old Baltimore,
   Heart-filled, head-filled with glee,
I saw a Baltimorean
   Keep looking straight at me.

Now I was eight and very small,
   And he was no whit bigger,
And so I smiled, but he poked out
   His tongue, and called me, "Nigger."

I saw the whole of Baltimore
   From May until December;
Of all the things that happened there
   That's all that I remember.

COUNTEE CULLEN

FIRST SONG

Then it was dusk in Illinois, the small boy
After an afternoon of carting dung
Hung on the rail fence, a sapped thing
Weary to crying. Dark was growing tall
And he began to hear the pond frogs all
Calling on his ear with what seemed their joy.

Soon their sound was pleasant for a boy
Listening in the smoky dust and the nightfall
Of Illinois, and from the fields two small
Boys came bearing cornstalk violins
And they rubbed the cornstalk bows with resins
And the three sat there scraping of their joy.

It was now fine music the frogs and the boys
Did in the towering Illinois twilight make
And into dark in spite of a shoulder's ache
A boy's hunched body loved out of a stalk
The first song of his happiness, and the song woke
His heart to the darkness and into the sadness of joy.

GALWAY KINNELL

WELL,
SON,
I'LL
TELL
YOU

MOTHER TO SON

Well, son, I'll tell you:
Life for me ain't been no crystal stair.
It's had tacks in it,
And splinters,
And boards torn up,
And places with no carpet on the floor—
Bare.
But all the time
I'se been a-climbin' on,
And reachin' landin's,
And turnin' corners,
And sometimes goin' in the dark
Where there ain't been no light.
So, boy, don't you turn back.
Don't set down on the steps
'Cause you find it kinder hard.
Don't you fall now—
For I'se still goin', honey,
I'se still climbin',
And life for me ain't been no crystal stair.

LANGSTON HUGHES

THOSE WINTER SUNDAYS

Sundays too my father got up early
and put his clothes on in the blueblack cold,
then with cracked hands that ached
from labor in the weekday weather made
banked fires blaze. No one ever thanked him.

I'd wake and hear the cold splintering, breaking.
When the rooms were warm, he'd call,
and slowly I would rise and dress,
fearing the chronic angers of that house.

Speaking indifferently to him,
who had driven out the cold
and polished my good shoes as well.
What did I know, what did I know
of love's austere and lonely offices?

ROBERT HAYDEN

MY PAPA'S WALTZ

The whiskey on your breath
Could make a small boy dizzy;
But I hung on like death:
Such waltzing was not easy.

We romped until the pans
Slid from the kitchen shelf;
My mother's countenance
Could not unfrown itself.

The hand that held my wrist
Was battered on one knuckle;
At every step you missed
My right ear scraped a buckle.

You beat time on my head
With a palm caked hard by dirt,
Then waltzed me off to bed
Still clinging to your shirt.

THEODORE ROETHKE

CIVILIZING THE CHILD

You can't keep it, I say,
it will decay.
Bury the mouse, I tell her,
it will make the tulips redder,
give the trees babies,
fatten the faces of daisies,
put manes on the grass.
Spring comes up thick from the dead, I say,
broadcasting words like seeds
until she obeys, sadly,
with her green child's trowel.
And when she runs out the next morning
to see if the pink hawthorn
has an extra blossom or two
—and it has, it has!—
I go scot-free, acquitted
by her happiness-tinged cheeks,
my judges, my blind jury.

LISEL MUELLER

VACATION TRIP

The loudest thing in our car
was Mother being glum:

> Little chiding valves
> a surge of detergent oil
> all that deep chaos
> the relentless accurate fire
> the drive shaft wild to arrive

And tugging along behind in its great big
balloon, that looming piece in her mind:

"I wish I hadn't come."

WILLIAM STAFFORD

DIVORCE

Papa finally left us
to cause a fuss in a different house
browbeat a different wife
pound his fists on a different table
I thought

But when I went to their place one day
to visit
(though I didn't really want to)
Papa anxiously rushed around
taking orders
from that cat-like lady
And their son
newborn
was the apple of his eye

SIV WIDERBERG
Translated by Verne Moberg

LEGACIES

her grandmother called her from the playground
   "yes, ma'am"
   "i want chu to learn how to make rolls" said the old
woman proudly
but the little girl didn't want
to learn how because she knew
even if she couldn't say it that
that would mean when the old one died she would be less
dependent upon her spirit so
she said
   "i don't want to know how to make no rolls"
with her lips poked out
and the old woman wiped her hands on
her apron saying "lord
   these children"
and neither of them ever
said what they meant
and i guess nobody ever does

NIKKI GIOVANNI

THE PORTRAIT

My mother never forgave my father
for killing himself,
especially at such an awkward time
and in a public park,
that spring
when I was waiting to be born.
She locked his name
in her deepest cabinet
and would not let him out,
though I could hear him thumping.
When I came down from the attic
with the pastel portrait in my hand
of a long-lipped stranger
with a brave moustache
and deep brown level eyes,
she ripped it into shreds
without a single word
and slapped me hard.
In my sixty-fourth year
I can feel my cheek
still burning.

STANLEY KUNITZ

MOTHERS

the last time i was home
to see my mother we kissed
exchanged pleasantries
and unpleasantries pulled a warm
comforting silence around
us and read separate books

i remember the first time
i consciously saw her
we were living in a three room
apartment on burns avenue

mommy always sat in the dark
i don't know how she knew but she did

that night i stumbled into the kitchen
maybe because i've always been
a night person or perhaps because i had wet
the bed
she was sitting on a chair
the room was bathed in moonlight diffused through
those thousands of panes landlords who rented
to people with children were prone to put in windows

she may have been smoking but maybe not
her hair was three-quarters her height
which made me a strong believer in the samson myth
and very black

she was very deliberately waiting
perhaps for my father to come home
from his night job or maybe for a dream

that had promised to come by
"come here" she said "i'll teach you
a poem: *i see the moon*
the moon sees me
god bless the moon
and god bless me"
i taught it to my son
who recited it for her
just to say we must learn
to bear the pleasures
as we have borne the pains

NIKKI GIOVANNI

NIÑO LEADING AN OLD MAN TO MARKET

He is leading his grandfather under the sun to market.
Who needs to see? The hand is warm on his shoulder.
The sun tells a man whatever he has to know
And the eyes of the children take care of the rest.

This is a little procession, solemn and steady,
A way of seeing that has the right direction,
And needs the simplest of eyes; the hand is quite sure,
And the wealth of the sun takes care of the rest.

His children have children to spare for any errand
An old man must go on; like sun, they are warmly with him,
Though at night his wakeful hand may remember that seeing
Was going alone in any direction.

Time takes care of the rest. In the niño's eyes
He is leading his grandfather under the sun to market.
In the old man's mind he walks through warmth where he
    must.
They are going in one direction, and know it.

LEONARD NATHAN

I MET
AN
ADOLESCENT
KITTEN
ON
LEXINGTON
AVE.

EASTSIDE CHICK WITH DRIVE

I met an adolescent kitten on Lexington Ave.
    one day—
  A fragile little thing,
Apricot, with a proud chest, soft, quick ears,
  Funny feet, frank eyes,
I said, "What are you doing out on your own
Among traffic lights and trucks
  Dumb dogs and careless kids?
You'll get chased down alleys,
  Stained, used, tossed aside.
The world's real!"

"I know there's risk," she said,
  "But I'm built for all that, maybe,
To be stained, used, tossed aside.
  I'm bored dreaming out of windows,
  Dozing in chairs, waiting.
  And I'm so clean!"

She wished me luck and darted into Zum Zum's.
Last I heard, she went to a college upstate.

ALBERT SPECTOR

PORTRAIT OF A GIRL WITH COMIC BOOK

Thirteen's no age at all. Thirteen is nothing.
It is not wit, or powder on the face,
Or Wednesday matinees, or misses' clothing,
Or intellect, or grace.
Twelve has its tribal customs. But thirteen
is neither boys in battered cars nor dolls,
Not *Sara Crewe* or movie magazine,
Or pennants on the wall.

Thirteen keeps diaries and tropical fish
(a month, at most); scorns jumpropes in the spring;
Could not, would fortune grant it, name a wish;
Wants nothing, everything;
Has secrets from itself, friends it despises;
Admits none of the terrors that it feels;
Owns half a hundred masks but no disguises;
And walks upon its heels.

Thirteen's anomalous—not that, not this:
Not folded bud, or wave that laps a shore,
Or moth proverbial from the chrysalis.
Is the one age that defeats metaphor.
Is not a town, like childhood, strongly walled
But easily surrendered; it is not city.
Nor, quitted once, can it be quite recalled—
Not even with pity.

PHYLLIS MC GINLEY

JAKE HATES ALL THE GIRLS

jake hates
        all the girls(the
shy ones,the bold
ones;the meek
proud sloppy sleek)
all except the cold
               ones

paul scorns all
        the girls(the
bright ones;the dim
ones;the slim
plump tiny tall)
all except the
          dull ones

gus loves all the
          girls(the
warped ones;the lamed
ones;the mad
moronic maimed)
all except
       the dead ones

mike likes all the girls
           (the
fat ones,the lean
ones;the mean
kind dirty clean)
all
  except the green ones

E. E. CUMMINGS

49

AUGUST AFTERNOON

I remember the August afternoon
we washed the seats
in the '66 bug
with buckets of water, soap, and brushes.
Feeling a little like Cinderella
I crawled in on my hands and knees
and started to scrub
while soapy dirt ran
down my arms and legs
and sweat dripped off my hair.
I threw water on you
and in return I got
a dripping wet cloth in my face:
the battle was on.
Grimy grey water splashed over us
as we chased each other
with sponges and brushes.
We went back to work
drenched and laughing
only to emerge an hour later
looking old and prunish.
Then, like Jack and Jill
we carried our buckets
back to the house
and on the way
you said thanks
I love you.

NANCY REMALY

THE PICNIC

It is the picnic with Ruth in the spring.
Ruth was third on my list of seven girls
But the first two were gone (Betty) or else
Had someone (Ellen has accepted Doug).
Indian Gully the last day of school;
Girls make the lunches for the boys too.
I wrote a note to Ruth in algebra class
Day before the test. She smiled, and nodded.
We left the cars and walked through the young corn
The shoots green as paint and the leaves like tongues
Trembling. Beyond the fence where we stood
Some wild strawberry flowered by an elm tree
and Jack-in-the pulpit was olive ripe.
A blackbird fled as I crossed, and showed
A spot of gold or red under its quick wing.
I held the wire for Ruth and watched the whip
Of her long, striped skirt as she followed.
Three freckles blossomed on her thin, white back
Underneath the loop where the blouse buttoned.
We went for our lunch away from the rest,
Stretched in new grass, our heads close
Over unknown things wrapped up in wax papers.
Ruth tried for the same, I forget what it was,
And our hands were together. She laughed,
And a breeze caught the edge of her little
Collar and the edge of her brown, loose hair
That touched my cheek. I turned my face in-
to the gentle fall. I saw how sweet it smelled.
She didn't move her head or take her hand.
I felt a soft caving in my stomach
As at the top of the highest slide
When I had been a child, but was not afraid,
And did not know why my eyes moved with wet

As I brushed her cheek with my lips and brushed
Her lips with my own lips. She said to me
Jack, Jack, different than I had ever heard
Because she wasn't calling me, I think,
Or telling me. She used my name to
Talk in another way and then she took her hand;
I gave her what we both had touched—can't
Remember what it was, and we ate the lunch.
Afterward we walked in the small, cool creek
Our shoes off, her skirt hitched, and she smiling,
My pants rolled, and then we climbed up the high
Side of Indian Gully and looked
Where we had been, our hands together again.
It was then some bright thing came in my eyes,
Starting at the back of them and flowing
Suddenly through my head and down my arms
And stomach and my bare legs that seemed not
To stop in feet, not to feel the red earth
Of the Gully, as though we hung in a
Touch of birds. There was a word in my throat
With the feeling and I knew the first time
What it meant and I said, it's beautiful.
Yes, she said, and I felt the sound and word
In my hand join the sound and word in hers
As in one name said, or in one cupped hand.
We put back on our shoes and socks and we
Sat in the grass awhile, crosslegged, under
A blowing tree, not saying anything.
And Ruth played with shells she found in the creek,
As I watched. Her small wrist which was so sweet
To me turned by her breast and the shells dropped
Green, white, blue, easily into her lap,
Passing light through themselves. She gave the pale
Shells to me, and got up and touched her hips
With her light hands, and we walked down slowly
To play the school games with the others.

53

JOHN LOGAN

TO KATE, SKATING BETTER THAN HER DATE

Wait, Kate! You skate at such a rate
You leave behind your skating mate.
Your splendid speed won't you abate?
He's lagging far behind you, Kate.
He brought you on this skating date
His shy affection thus to state,
But you on skating concentrate
And leave him with a woeful weight
Pressed on his heart. Oh, what a state
A man gets into, how irate
He's bound to be with life and fate
If, when he tries to promulgate
His love, the loved one turns to skate
Far, far ahead to demonstrate
Superior speed and skill. Oh, hate
Is sure to come of love, dear Kate,
If you so treat your skating mate.
Turn again, Kate, or simply wait
Until he comes, then him berate
(Coyly) for catching up so late.
For, Kate, he *knows* your skating's great,
He's *seen* your splendid figure eight,
He is not here to contemplate
Your supersonic skating rate—
That is not why he made the date.
He's anxious to expatiate
On how he wants you for his mate.
And don't you want to hear him, Kate?

DAVID DAICHES

54

PUERTO RICANS IN NEW YORK   I

She enters the bus demurely
with the delicate dark face
the Spaniards first saw
on an island in the Caribbean
and he follows—
a tall gentle lad.
He smiles pleasantly, shyly,
at her now and then,
but she does not look at him,
looking away demurely.
She holds a small package in her hand—
perhaps a nightgown—
and he a larger package:
a brand-new windowshade.

CHARLES REZNIKOFF

THE YAWN

The black-haired girl
with the big
      brown
          eyes
on the Queen's train coming
       in to work, so
opens her mouth so beautifully
     wide
         in a ya-aawn, that
two stops after she has left the train
I have only to think of her   and I
               o-oh-aaaww—hm
               wow   !

PAUL BLACKBURN

The pennycandystore beyond the El
is where I first
                fell in love
                        with unreality
Jellybeans glowed in the semi-gloom
of that september afternoon
A cat upon the counter moved among
                the licorice sticks
            and tootsie rolls
        and Oh Boy Gum

Outside the leaves were falling as they died
A wind had blown away the sun

A girl ran in
Her hair was rainy
Her breasts were breathless in the little room
                        .
Outside the leaves were falling
                and they dried
                        Too soon! too soon!

LAWRENCE FERLINGHETTI

RECUERDO

We were very tired, we were very merry—
We had gone back and forth all night on the ferry.
It was bare and bright, and smelled like a stable—
But we looked into a fire, we leaned across a table,
We lay on a hill-top underneath a moon;
And the whistles kept blowing, and the dawn came soon.

We were very tired, we were very merry—
We had gone back and forth all night on the ferry;
And you ate an apple, and I ate a pear,
From a dozen of each we had bought somewhere;
And the sky went wan, and the wind came cold,
And the sun rose dripping, a bucketful of gold.

We were very tired, we were very merry.
We had gone back and forth all night on the ferry.
We hailed, "Good-morrow, mother!" to a shawl-covered head,
And bought a morning paper, which neither of us read;
And she wept, "God bless you!" for the apples and the pears,
And we gave her all our money but our subway fares.

EDNA ST. VINCENT MILLAY

I BET
WE
LOOK
MARRIED

ARCHES AND SHADOWS

He proposed to me on the Ferris wheel—
I nearly fell off!—and once we dived
off the board holding hands, I remember,
though not very clearly. O it may not have been
croquet on the lawn and twenty for dinner,
but we had our times, sir, and I had mine,
awaiting election returns with the old crowd
before I left. In Trieste I said Promise
you'll always love me, I actually said that,
and at the fair in Brussels I made
an extremely witty remark. A white puppy
followed me all one afternoon, all
around the race track. He promised;
he said we would live in a houseboat—
raise ponies—sell apples—dry flowers—
all this in a peat-fire pub on Exmoor;
I was sunburned all over, even my hands.
Now in November when the cat wants out early,
it's your face I see in the folds of my dress on the chair.
I'll meet you in March in Alberta;
today I sewed a pleat and cut a lemon in your name,
thinking: then I will travel the Great Northern Railways
and we can talk things over, sitting down.

ANNIE DILLARD

THE COUPLE

A Greek ship
Sails on the sea
Carrying me past
The islands
Into an unknown
Island where
The burros
Are sleeping, houses
Are white, and brown
Honey is sold in
The general store. That's
Me up on the hill
Living with the
Man I'm going
To marry—there
We are—he plays
The violin
But never practices,
I fold and unfold
The nylon blouses
I brought from
America and put
Them neatly in
A drawer. It is
Time to go out.
We explore the island
And at the same time
Argue about
Getting married.
We walk close to
The sea, which happens
To knock our eyes

Out with its blue. An
Old lady, call her a
Witch, passes us by and
Asks us the way to
The post office.
We continue on the rocks,
Walking by the sea. "I bet
We look married," I say,
And turn my eyes from
The sea. "Only to
An old lady
Going to mail
Letters at the post
Office," he replies
And begins to weep.
Not one snorkel
Will float
Us under the sea,
To the schools of fish
Who are enjoying
Their mateless
Existence, or
Take us away from
Our troubles. The
Young girl folds
Up her blouses and
Begins to pack.
The young man
Picks up his fiddle
And places it
Back into
The imitation
Alligator case.
The island
Now is sinking
Beneath the blue sea.

The life plot thickens.
Wait.
We have forgotten
Our footsteps.
We must
Cover them up
To
The post office.

SANDRA HOCHMAN

POEM FOR LORRY

At the bottom of the twisted
stairs, under fern and blackberry
bushes, I sat in pine shade
on a bark-stripped log
and scribbled poems.
Yesterday I heard light steps
on the stairs above, branches
moved behind me. I'm writing,
I said without turning around.
She left quickly but I felt
her absence in the poem.
The notebook shut, I climbed
to the house. She was on the bed
crying.

GERALD HAUSMAN

LIARD HOT SPRINGS

We were up before anyone,
walking the long planks
to the steaming water.
This was our time.
We did everything
that we would do alone.
Water poured over the rocks,
steam rose,
I washed your long back
with white soap.
This was the only way that we would have it.
We did not even know
then
that you were pregnant,
and it didn't matter.
We were alone.
We belonged to each other.
We were like two fish
darting
in and out of the water
before dawn.

GORDON MASSMAN

FOR A MARRIAGE
(seven years old, just beginning)

After we had torn out
each other's ribs
& put them back—

after we had juggled thigh bones
& knee caps
& tossed each other's skulls at friends,

after we had sucked
each other's blood
& spat it out,

after we had sucked
each other's blood
& swallowed it
licking our lips—

after the betrayals
& imagined betrayals—

after you left me in the snow
& I left you in the rain
& we both came back—

after staying together
out of lust
& out of fear
& out of laziness—

we find ourselves
entangled in each other's arms,

grown into each other
like Siamese twins,
embedded in each other
like ingrown toenails,

& for the first time
wanting each other
only.

ERICA JONG

I'M
MAKIN'
A
ROAD

FLORIDA ROAD WORKERS

I'm makin' a road
For the cars to fly by on,
Makin' a road
Through the palmetto thicket
For light and civilization
To travel on.

I'm makin' a road
For the rich to sweep over
In their big cars
And leave me standin' here.

Sure,
A road helps everybody!
Rich folks ride—
And I get to see 'em ride.

I ain't never seen nobody
Ride so fine before.
Hey, Buddy. Look!
I'm makin' a road!

LANGSTON HUGHES

TRUCK DRIVERS

At two a.m.,
the sad-eyed conquerors sit
hunched in familiar
leatherette booths,
waiting for the weariness
to pass,
waiting to be on their roads again.
Their honky music
hangs in the air
like yesterday's cigar smoke,
and the songs are about
themselves.
They talk together
like long-time companions,
knowing they may never
meet again,
and knowing it doesn't matter.
They've met themselves
a million times
in a million roadside,
run-down cafes,
drunk countless cups of
black, bitter coffee,
talked countless conquests
of roads and women.
The stories are all the same,
and only the faces
have been changed.
Men of the black mainstreams
of America,
you know this land
from smoky, sprawling city

to silent two-house towns,
you know this land.
Crossing, recrossing and night highways,
delivering America's
abundance,
you've learned the maps
by heart.
Sad-eyed conquerors,
drink your coffee,
think of home.

TERRI HAAG

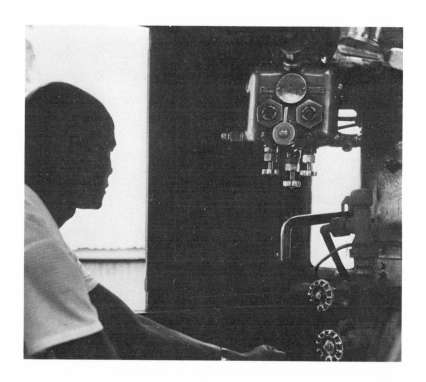

MUCKERS

Twenty men stand watching the muckers.
  Stabbing the sides of the ditch
  Where clay gleams yellow,
  Driving the blades of their shovels
  Deeper and deeper for the new gas mains,
  Wiping sweat off their faces
    With red bandanas.

The muckers work on . . . pausing . . . to pull
Their boots out of suckholes where they slosh.

  Of the twenty looking on
Ten murmur, "O, it's a hell of a job."
Ten others, "Jesus, I wish I had a job."

CARL SANDBURG

COONEY POTTER

I inherited forty acres from my Father
And, by working my wife, my two sons and two daughters
From dawn to dusk, I acquired
A thousand acres. But not content,
Wishing to own two thousand acres,
I bustled through the years with axe and plow,
Toiling, denying myself, my wife, my sons, my daughters.
Squire Higbee wrongs me to say
That I died from smoking Red Eagle cigars.
Eating hot pie and gulping coffee
During the scorching hours of harvest time
Brought me here ere I had reached my sixtieth year.

EDGAR LEE MASTERS

VERMONT CONVERSATION

"Good weather for hay."
  "Yes, 'tis."
"Mighty bright day."
  "That's true."
"Crops comin' on?"
  "Yep. You?"
"Tol'rable; beans got the blight."
  "Way o' the Lord."
"That's right."

PATRICIA HUBBELL

HAY FOR THE HORSES

He had driven half the night
From far down San Joaquin
Through Mariposa, up the
Dangerous mountain roads,
And pulled in at eight a.m.
With his big truckload of hay
    behind the barn.
With winch and ropes and hooks
We stacked the bales up clean
To splintery redwood rafters
High in the dark, flecks of alfalfa
Whirling through shingle-cracks of light,
Itch of haydust in the
    sweaty shirt and shoes.
At lunchtime under Black oak
Out in the hot corral,
—The old mare nosing lunchpails,
Grasshoppers crackling in the weeds—
'I'm sixty-eight,' he said,
'I first bucked hay when I was seventeen.
I thought, that day I started,
I sure would hate to do this all my life.
And dammit, that's just what
I've gone and done.'

GARY SNYDER

EX-BASKETBALL PLAYER

Pearl Avenue runs past the high-school lot,
Bends with the trolley tracks, and stops, cut off
Before it has a chance to go two blocks,
At Colonel McComsky Plaza. Berth's Garage
Is on the corner facing west, and there
Most days, you'll find Flick Webb, who helps Berth out.

Flick stands tall among the idiot pumps—
Five on a side, the old bubble-head style,
Their rubber elbows hanging loose and low.
One's nostrils are two S's, and his eyes
An E and O. And one is squat, without
A head at all—more of a football type.

Once Flick played for the high-school team, the Wizards.
He was good: in fact, the best. In '46
He bucketed three hundred ninety points,
A county record still. The ball loved Flick.
I saw him rack up thirty-eight of forty
In one home game. His hands were like wild birds.

He never learned a trade, he just sells gas,
Checks oil, and changes flats. Once in a while,
As a gag, he dribbles an inner tube,
But most of us remember anyway.
His hands are fine and nervous on the lug wrench.
It makes no difference to the lug wrench, though.

Off work, he hangs around Mae's Luncheonette,
Grease-gray and kind of coiled, he plays pinball,
Sips lemon cokes, and smokes those thin cigars;
Flick seldom speaks to Mae, just sits and nods
Beyond her face towards bright applauding tiers
Of Necco Wafers, Nibs, and Juju Beads.

82

JOHN UPDIKE

THE PAPER CUTTER

He slides the cut paper out
from under the raised knife.
His face does not lose interest.
"And now I go to my night job,"
he says cheerfully at five,
wiping his hands upon a rag.
He has stood all day in one spot,
pressing first the left
and then the right button.
"And what are you going to do
with all that money?" I ask.
His shoulders stick out bony.
"I will buy a house
and then I will lie down in it
and not get up all day," he laughs.

DAVID IGNATOW

V. B. NIMBLE, V. B. QUICK

Science, Pure and Applied, by V. B. Wigglesworth, F.R.S.,
Quick Professor of Biology in the University of Cambridge.
—*A talk listed in the B.B.C. Radio Times of February 2, 1955.*

V. B. Wigglesworth wakes at noon,
Washes, shaves, and very soon
Is at the lab; he reads his mail,
Swings a tadpole by the tail,
Undoes his coat, removes his hat
Dips a spider in a vat
Of alkaline, phones the press,
Tells them he is F.R.S.,
Subdivides six protocells,
Kills a rat by ringing bells,
Writes a treatise, edits two
Symposia on "Will Man Do?,"
Gives a lecture, audits three,
Has the Sperm Club in for tea,
Pensions off an aging spore,
Cracks a test tube, takes some pure
Science and applies it, finds
His hat, adjusts it, pulls the blinds,
Instructs the jellyfish to spawn,
And, by one o'clock, he's gone.

JOHN UPDIKE

THE RETURN TO WORK

Promenading their
skirted galleons of sex,
the two office assistants

rock unevenly
together
down the broad stairs,

one
(as I follow slowly
in the trade wind

of my admiration)
gently
slapping her thighs.

WILLIAM CARLOS WILLIAMS

THE STORY-TELLER

He talked, and as he talked
Wallpaper came alive;
Suddenly ghosts walked,
And four doors were five;

Calendars ran backward,
And maps had mouths;
Ships went tackward
In a great drowse;

Trains climbed trees
And soon dipped down
Like honey of bees
On the cold brick town.

He had wakened a worm
In the world's brain,
And nothing stood firm
Until day again.

MARK VAN DOREN

YOU GOTTA LIVE
TO BE
SEVENTY-NINE
FORE YOU
CAN
UNDERSTAND
ANYHOW

MODEL T

The hill was higher every year,
the old car older, less adept
at climbing up a road designed
to haul all climbers back to earth.

My grandfather pressed his muddy shoe
against the narrow, shaken floor,
and cursed the engineer who made
the world too steep. I cheered
from my safe nest behind,
where storm curtains gasped like leather birds
(in love with engines, mountains, games),
while my grandmother rocked her ridden weight
against the gravity of things,
relying on her will to aid
the long futility of iron.

We coasted down the other side
where yellow fields made a long sea.
I yearned for something tall again,
sky-scorched and wild—
then heard her wrinkled sigh
and saw his hands, grease-etched and gray,
grapple with pride
the thin and perilous wheel.

ADRIEN STOUTENBURG

MANNERS
For a Child of 1918

My grandfather said to me
as we sat on the wagon seat,
"Be sure to remember to always
speak to everyone you meet."

We met a stranger on foot.
My grandfather's whip tapped his hat.
"Good day, sir. Good day. A fine day."
And I said it and bowed where I sat.

Then we overtook a boy we knew
with his pet crow on his shoulder.
"Always offer everyone a ride;
don't forget that when you get older,"

my grandfather said. So Willy
climbed up with us, but the crow
gave a "Caw!" and flew off. I was worried.
How would he know where to go?"

But he flew a little way at a time
from fence post to fence post, ahead;
and when Willy whistled he answered.
"A fine bird," my grandfather said,

"and he's well brought up. See, he answers
nicely when he's spoken to.
Man or beast, that's good manners.
Be sure that you both always do."

When automobiles went by,
the dust hid the people's faces,

but we shouted "Good day! Good day!
Fine day!" at the top of our voices.

When we came to Hustler Hill,
he said that the mare was tired,
so we all got down and walked,
as our good manners required.

ELIZABETH BISHOP

AUNT ALICE IN APRIL

By mid-day it was warm enough; she climbed
The path up through the orchard, stopping twice
To catch her breath and give her heart a rest.
Just to the left there somewhere, past the rock
Shaped like a sugar-loaf, the child had found
The bloodroot blooming and had stained her hands.

It was no use; her eyesight was too weak.
She could not find them and she dared not kneel
With no one there to help her up. She sighed
And peered around her at the feathering leaves.

Yes, it was truly spring once more.
                                   She turned
And made her slow way back to the house.

WILLIAM H. MATCHETT

THE RAINWALKERS

An old man whose black face
shines golden-brown as wet pebbles
under the streetlamp, is walking
two mongrel dogs of dis-
proportionate size, in the rain,
in the relaxed early-evening avenue.

The small sleek one wants to stop,
docile to the imploring soul of the trashbasket,
but the young tall curly one
wants to walk on; the glistening sidewalk
entices him to arcane happenings.

Increasing rain. The old bareheaded man
smiles and grumbles to himself.
The lights change: the avenue's
endless nave echoes notes of
liturgical red. He drifts

between his dogs' desires.
The three of them are enveloped—
turning now to go crosstown—in their
sense of each other, of pleasure,
of weather, of corners,
of leisurely tensions between them
and private silence.

DENISE LEVERTOV

LONELINESS

I was about to go, and said so;
And I had almost started for the door.
But he was all alone in the sugar-house,
And more lonely than he'd ever been before.
We'd talked for half an hour, almost,
About the price of sugar, and how I like my school,
And he had made me drink some syrup hot,
Telling me it was better that way than when cool.

And I agreed, and thanked him for it,
And said good-bye, and was about to go.
Want to see where I was born?
He asked me quickly. How to say no?

The sugar-house looked over miles of valley.
He pointed with a sticky finger to a patch of snow
Where he was born. The house, he said, was gone.
I understand these people better, now I know.

BROOKS JENKINS

The old woman sits
Everyday on the porch, waiting.
She sits rocking
back and forth.
Time has no meaning to her.
Not any more.
Her worn and tough hands
are never without
the knitting needles.
She knits the only warmth
she will receive all winter.

LEASA DAVIS

OLD FLORIST

That hump of a man bunching chrysanthemums
Or pinching-back asters, or planting azaleas,
Tamping and stamping dirt into pots—
How he could flick and pick
Rotten leaves or yellow petals,
Or scoop out a weed close to flourishing roots,
Or make the dust buzz with a light spray,
Or drown a bug in one spit of tobacco juice,
Or fan life into wilted sweet-peas with his hat,
Or stand all night watering roses, his feet blue
    in rubber boots.

THEODORE ROETHKE

HOW TUESDAY BEGAN

Don't let me lose you,
lady. We're jogging up
First Avenue in the sun,
nursing morning with
our habits.
I must have boarded before
you, where the bus stops
and the dusty nightgowns
beckon from Orchard St.
I must have pulled out
my book, peeled off my gloves,
and settled among the fumes
for a poem or two,
my habit.
I didn't see you,
black, filling the aisle
with your green housedress,
lowering each part of you
gently, in front of me,
maybe heaving a sigh, your
sorrow and habit.

Still, my eyes pulled
sideways. Someone old
moved without moving,
veins, vague eyes resisting
the aisle in front
of her, a journey
to be mastered upright,
seat by seat.

We rolled with the bus,
easy as rubber lifeboats

on troubled water.
But she hung to the same
space, sensing the movement
around her, sinking
in her own flesh.
Then you reached out, lady,
and pulled her in
beside you.
You were fading
and full of troubles, lady,
and you saw her drowning
and you reached out
and said, "I don't see
so good myself."

KATHLEEN FRASER

OLD PEOPLE

It beats me. The way
They sit there talking
Day after day.

   Mrs. Lotts was married twice.
   Her first husband lives in Sioux City.
   Remember John Coleman?
   He doesn't have a nickel.
   My, your new dress looks nice!
   That young Hodges girl is pretty.
   Ruth gave me a recipe for a new kind of pickle.

(And heaven knows what all—)
Irma got sick. The Johnstones moved away.
Teddy is coming to visit. Lucille put new carpet in her hall.
Louise called the doctor three times yesterday.

It beats me. The way
They sit there talking
Day after day.
Arms folded, ankles crossed,
Talking and talking and talking and talking and talking.

MYRA COHN LIVINGSTON

CONVERSATION

"yeah" she said "my man's gone too
been dead longer than you is old"
"what do you do" i asked
"sit here on the porch and talk to the old folk
i rock and talk and go to church most times"
"but aren't you lonely sometimes" i asked
"now you gotta answer yo own question"
"i guess the children help a lot   you got grandchildren
haven't you"
"oh the children they come and go always in a hurry
got something to do ain't no time for old folks
like me"
she squinted at the sun packing her jaw
with *bruton* snuff
"the old days done gone . . . and i say goodbye
people be going to the moon and all . . . ain't that
wonderful . . . to the moon"
and i said "i see stars all the time aretha franklin
and sly were at madison square garden recently"
"what you doing there" she asked
"i'm a poet" i said
"that ain't no reason to be uppity"
and the sun beat down on my head while
a dragonfly admonished my flippancy
but a blue and yellow butterfly sat on my knee
i looked her square in the eye
"i ain't gonna tell you" she said and turned her head
"ain't gonna tell me what" i asked
"what you asking me you gotta live to be seventy-nine
fore you can understand anyhow"
"now you being uppity" i said
"yeah but i earned it" she replied and shifting her wad

she clapped her hands and smiled
"you been here before"
and i said "yes ma'am but would you tell me just one thing
what did i learn"
and she spat out her juice
"honey if you don't know how can i"
i wanted to argue but the sun was too hot and the sky
too lazy and god heaved a sigh that swept under my blouse
and i felt me feeling a feeling
she crossed her legs at the ankle
and straightened her back
"tell you this" she said
"keep yo dress up and yo pants down and you'll be all right"
and i said impatiently "old lady you got it all wrong"
"honey, ain't never been wrong yet
you better get back to the city cause you one of them
technical niggers and you'll have problems here"

NIKKI GIOVANNI

PHONE CALL TO RUTHERFORD

"It would be—
    a mercy if
you did not come to see me . . .

"I have dif-fi   /   culty
    speak-ing, I
cannot count on it, I
am afraid it would be too em-
    ba
    rass-ing
for me   "

    —Bill, can you still
    answer letters?
"No   my hands
are tongue-tied   You have . . . made

a record in my heart.
    Goodbye."

PAUL BLACKBURN

"I'm 92," Joe said,
 eyes surprised
 like he heard his age
 for the first time.
His words were quiet
 like Monterey fog.
He was thin as a trolling spar,
 arms hung taut
 as trolling lines,
 with a leaden weight
 of wasted years
 in each hand.
Harsh winds, burning sun
 and smoldering dreams
 charred his face.
But his fingers were still nimble
 for mending nets.
"I go down to the bay every day
 to make sure the boats are still there."
The canner tapped his forehead:
 "Joe was one of my best fishermen,"
 he said, tapping his head again.
"Lost his son in the war.
Been a little off ever since.
Sometimes he sits down there on the dock
 and talks to a seagull."
"Sometimes I talk to a seagull," Joe said.

TOM WEBER

ELEGY

Her face like a rain-beaten stone on the day she rolled off
With the dark hearse, and enough flowers for an alderman,—
And so she was, in her way, Aunt Tilly.

Sighs, sighs, who says they have sequence?
Between the spirit and the flesh,—what war?
She never knew;
For she asked no quarter and gave none,
Who sat with the dead when the relatives left,
Who fed and tended the infirm, the mad, the epileptic,
And, with a harsh rasp of a laugh at herself,
Faced up to the worst.

I recall how she harried the children away all the late summer
From the one beautiful thing in her yard, the peachtree;
How she kept the wizened, the fallen, the misshapen for
    herself,
And picked and pickled the best, to be left on rickety
    doorsteps.

And yet she died in agony,
Her tongue, at the last, thick, black as an ox's.

Terror of cops, bill collectors, betrayers of the poor,—
I see you in some celestial supermarket,
Moving serenely among the leeks and cabbages,
Probing the squash,
Bearing down with two steady eyes,
On the quaking butcher.

THEODORE ROETHKE

I SIT
AND LOOK OUT
UPON
ALL
THE SORROWS
OF THE
WORLD

I sit and look out upon all the sorrows of the world, and upon
    all oppressions and shame,
I hear secret convulsive sobs from young men at anguish with
    themselves, remorseful after deeds done,
I see in low life the mother misued by her children, dying,
    neglected, gaunt, desperate,
I see the wife misused by her husband, I see the treacherous
    seducer of young women,
I mark the ranklings of jealousy and unrequited love attempted
    to be hid, I see these sights on the earth,
I see the workings of battle, pestilence, tyranny, I see martyrs
    and prisoners,
I observe a famine at sea, I observe the sailors casting lots
    who shall be kill'd to preserve the lives of the rest,
I observe the slights and degradations cast by arrogant persons
    upon laborers, the poor, and upon Negroes, and the like;
All these—all the meanness and agony without end I sitting
    look out upon,
See, hear, and am silent.

WALT WHITMAN

A young man, wearing a loose jacket of light brown with a
    yellow muffler tied loosely about his throat,
is singing loudly to himself
a Spanish song.

"In my country," he says in English, "sing all the time:
money, sing;
no money, sing."

Then he adds *staccato* as beginners in a language do:
"Doughnuts, five cents.
Four cents—no doughnut!
Coffee, five cents.
Four cents, no coffee!
Restaurant.
Come in, please!"
And he bows deeply.
"No money!"
And he draws back, hands lifted,
the indignation of owner and waiter on his face.

"Girl."
He takes off the hat he does not have
and looks earnestly into the eyes
    of a girl that isn't there;
then smiles and looks aside coyly.
"No money!"
And he turns away in disgust.
"Ah, tragic, tragic, tragic!"

CHARLES REZNIKOFF

THE ADDICT

Sleepmonger,
deathmonger,
with capsules in my palms each night,
eight at a time from sweet pharmaceutical bottles
I make arrangements for a pint-sized journey.
I'm the queen of this condition.
I'm an expert on making the trip
and now they say I'm an addict.
Now they ask why.
Why!

Don't they know
that I promised to die!
I'm keeping in practice.
I'm merely staying in shape.
The pills are the mother, but better,
every color as good as sour balls.
I'm on a diet from death.

Yes, I admit
it has gotten to be a bit of a habit—
blows eight at a time, socked in the eye,
hauled away by the pink, the orange,
the green and white goodnights.
I'm becoming something of a chemical
mixture.
That's it!

My supply
of tablets
has got to last for years and years.
I like them more than I like me.

Stubborn as hell, they won't let go.
It's a kind of marriage.
It's a kind of war
where I plant bombs inside
of myself.

Yes
I try
to kill myself in small amounts,
an innocuous occupation.
Actually I'm hung up on it.
But remember I don't make too much noise.
And frankly no one has to lug me out
and I don't stand there in my winding sheet.
I'm a little buttercup in my yellow nightie
eating my eight loaves in a row
and in a certain order as in
the laying on of hands
or the black sacrament.

It's a ceremony
but like any other sport
it's full of rules.
It's like a musical tennis match where
my mouth keeps catching the ball.
Then I lie on my altar
elevated by the eight chemical kisses.

What a lay me down this is
with two pink, two orange,
two green, two white goodnights.
Fee-fi-fo-fum—
Now I'm borrowed.
Now I'm numb.

ANNE SEXTON

TROUBLED WOMAN

She stands
In the quiet darkness,
This troubled woman
Bowed by
Weariness and pain
Like an
Autumn flower
In the frozen rain,
Like a
Wind-blown autumn flower
That never lifts its head
Again.

LANGSTON HUGHES

from DEPRESSION

simple soul, who so early in the morning when only the
    poorest go to work,
stood up in the subway and outshouting the noise:
    "Excuse me, ladies and gentlemen, I have a baby at home
    who is sick,
and I have no money, no job;" who did not have a box or cap
    to take coins—
only his hands,
and, seeing only faces turned away,
did not even go down the aisle as beggars do.

CHARLES REZNIKOFF

FROM ST. LUKE'S HOSPITAL
Good Samaritan

She comes on at night,
older than middle-aged, from the islands,
to answer the patients' bells
to see if it's worth disturbing an overworked nurse.
At first she was suspicious, cross,
expecting complaints and impositions,
soon tender and gentle,
concerned about requests for help with pain,
coming (without being asked)
with a blanket if it turned cold,
hoping, as she said goodbye
at the night's end, for a good day.
This morning she rushed in, frantic,
please, please could she look for the money
she had lost somehow, tending patients,
forty dollars that was not even hers.
She had kept it, in time-honored tradition,
in her bosom, and it must have fallen out
when she was thinking of someone else's needs.
She scrabbled in the wastebasket,
in the bedclothes, panted from room to room,
returned to mine with a friend. We said,
"Close the door, take off your clothes, and see
if it isn't still on you somewhere."
She did, revealing an overworked body,
wrinkled, scarred; found nothing; had to leave.
She's off now, for a week. I'll never know
if she found it or not; will remember
her kindness and her panic. O God,
here, as so often, I cannot help.
Let me not forget she is your child
and your concern makes mine as nothing.
All I can do, and this I do, is love, is pray.

122

MADELEINE L'ENGLE

Here I sit in my infested cubicle
with wall to wall roaches
the rhythm of dripping water
is my only music
Shattered
cracked plaster
dictates where I hang pictures
and the taped window panes
peeling paint
missing panes
are but outward symbols of
my inner ghetto.

THERESA GREENWOOD

BOWERY

Bums are the spirit of us parked in ratty old hotels.
Bums are what we have made of angels,
given them old clothes to wear
dirty beards and an alcoholic breath,
to lie sprawled on gutters at our feet
as sacrifices to our idols: power and money.

Bums ask themselves, Why dress and shave,
and be well mannered, studious and hard-working,
own home and debts, a bank account and business
friends when others more eager are doing it
successfully? All we want is the right
to sit propped up against a wall, drunk
and drooling, letting urine seep through
our clothes onto the sidewalk, we
unconscious or unconcerned.
                              We with no money
relax anyway, letting the world come in
on us in sidewalk spit on which we sprawl,
in kicks and jabs from cops, under open skies
in rain and snow. None of you dares do it,
and so you do not know what money means.
We who live on charity enjoy the pleasure
of your wealth, the long hours filled
with drunkenness.

DAVID IGNATOW

MINERS

The police are dragging for the bodies
Of miners in the black waters
Of the suburbs.

Below, some few
Crawl, searching, until they clasp
The fingers of the sea.

Somewhere,
Beyond ripples and drowsing woodchucks,
A strong man, alone,
Beats on the door of a grave, crying
Oh let me in.

Many women mount long stairs
Into the shafts,
And emerge in tottering palaces
Of abandoned cisterns.

In the middle of the night,
I can hear cars, moving on steep rails, colliding
Underground.

JAMES WRIGHT

FOR LAURENCE JONES

Faceless miner
He died at 23
While on picket duty
Shot to death by a scab
In the employ of Duke Power Co.

Receive him
Harlan County earth
And remember him well
Every black-lunged UMW man
Raise his coffin like a battle flag.

Cherish him
Harlan County woman
You fought at his side
And took your children to jail
Rather than return to your place in silence.

Faceless miner
He died at 23
While on picket duty
Shot to death by a scab
In the employ of Duke Power Co.

GARY KIZER

FEEDING THE LIONS

They come into
our neighborhood
with the sun
an army of
social workers
carrying briefcases
filled with lies
and stupid grins
Passing out relief
checks
and food stamps
hustling from one
apartment to another
so they can fill
their quota
and get back out
before dark.

NORMAN JORDAN

SPEAKING: THE HERO

I did not want to go.
They inducted me.

I did not want to die.
They called me yellow.

I tried to run away.
They courtmartialed me.

I did not shoot.
They said I had no guts.

They ordered the attack.
A shrapnel tore my guts.

I cried in pain.
They carried me to safety.

In safety I died.
They blew taps over me.

They crossed out my name
and buried me under a cross.

They made a speech in my hometown.
I was unable to call them liars.

They said I gave my life.
I had struggled to keep it.

They said I set an example.
I had tried to run.

They said they were proud of me.
I had been ashamed of them.

They said my mother should also be proud.
My mother cried.

I wanted to live.
They called me a coward.

I died a coward.
They called me a hero.

FELIX POLLAK

THE DISTANT DRUM

I am not a metaphor or symbol.
This you hear is not the wind in the trees,
Nor a cat being maimed in the street.
I am being maimed in the street.
It is I who weep, laugh, feel pain or joy,
Speak this because I exist.
This is my voice.
These words are my words,
My mouth speaks them,
My hand writes them—
I am a poet.
It is my fist you hear
Beating against your ear.

CALVIN C. HERNTON

IN
ALL
PEOPLE
I SEE
MYSELF

Crowds of men and women attired in the usual costumes, how
  curious you are to me!
On the ferry-boats the hundreds and hundreds that cross, re-
  turning home, are more curious to me than you suppose,
And you that shall cross from shore to shore years hence are
  more to me, and more in my meditations, than you might
  suppose.

WALT WHITMAN

POEM

you can look into my face
and all you see is a very old face.
  but I can see in my eyes
  a great handsome young man.
you can look into my face
and all you can see is a sad lonesome young man.
  but I can see in my eyes
  a happy cheerful young man.
you can look into my face
and all you can see is mean.
  but I can see in my eyes
  a nice, gentle, generous young man.

MIKE TODACHINE

SIMPLE SONG

When we are going toward someone we say
You are just like me
your thoughts are my brothers
word matches word
how easy to be together.

When we are leaving someone we say
how strange you are
we cannot communicate
we can never agree
how hard, hard and weary to be together.

We are not different nor alike
but each strange in his leather body
sealed in skin and reaching out clumsy hands
and loving is an act
that cannot outlive
the open hand
the open eye
the door in the chest standing open.

MARGE PIERCY

WITH THE DOOR OPEN

Something I want to communicate to you,
I keep my door open between us.
I am unable to say it,
I am happy only
with the door open between us.

DAVID IGNATOW

SONG FORM

Morning uptown, quiet on the street,
no matter the distinctions that can be
made, quiet, very quiet, on the street.
Sun's not even up, just some kid and me,
skating, both of us, at the early sun, and
amazed there is a grace for us, without our
having to smile to be tough, or be very pleasant
even to each other. Merely to be mere'ly to be

LE ROI JONES
(Imamu Amiri Baraka)

TO SATCH

Sometimes I feel like I will never stop
Just go on forever
Till one fine morning
I'm gonna reach up and grab me a handful of stars
Swing out my long, lean leg
And whip three hot strikes burning down the heavens
And look over at God and say
How about that!

SAMUEL ALLEN

MEET
THE
POETS

SAMUEL ALLEN (1917-   ) was born in Columbus, Ohio. He graduated from Fisk University and Harvard Law School. He has been particularly interested in African poetry since his days as a student at the Sorbonne in Paris after World War II when he met many African students and writers. With the help of the American poet, Richard Wright, who was living in Paris at the time, Allen had a number of his poems published in the French magazine, *Presence Africaine*, much of it under the pseudonym of Paul Vesey. Allen's poetry has been widely anthologized in the United States and abroad. Currently he is Professor of English at Boston University.

IMAMU AMIRI BARAKA (1934-   ) was born LeRoi Jones in Newark, New Jersey. He attended Rutgers, Howard, and Columbia Universities and the New School for Social Research in New York. His books of poetry include *Preface to a Twenty-Volume Suicide Note* (1961), *Black Magic* (1969), and *Spirit, Reach* (1972). He is the author of several plays, a study of Negro music in America entitled *Blues People* (1963), a novel, a volume of short stories, and numerous

147

magazine articles. As the founder of the Black Arts Repertory Theatre in Harlem and of Spirit House, a community organization of Newark, he has become a significant force in the Black Arts Movement of the United States.

ELIZABETH BISHOP (1911-   ) was born in Worcester, Massachusetts, and graduated from Vassar College. She has won several distinguished prizes for her poetry (including the Pulitzer Prize in 1956 and the National Book Award in 1969) and has served as the Poetry Consultant to the Library of Congress. From 1952-1967 she lived in Brazil, but she now makes her home in San Francisco.

PAUL BLACKBURN (1926-   ) was born in Vermont and graduated from the University of Wisconsin in 1950. He was a Fulbright scholar at the University of Toulouse, France, in 1954-55 and the following year was American lecturer at the same university. His poetry has appeared in numerous magazines and anthologies. His books include *Brooklyn-Manhattan Transit* (1960), *The Nets* (1961), *The Cities* (1967) and *In, On, or About the Premises* (1968).

JOHN CIARDI [*Chár-dey*] (1916-   ) was born in Boston and graduated from Tufts College and the University of Michigan. For many years an English professor (at Harvard and then Rutgers) and poetry editor of *Saturday Review*, he has received innumerable prizes and awards for his poetic translation of Dante, his poetry for adults, and his critical commentary on the nature of poetry. His first books of poetry for children grew out of play with his small nephew and his own children. Ciardi is quoted as saying "I dislike most of the children's poems I see because they seem written by a sponge dipped in warm milk and sprinkled with sugar." By contrast, his poetry for children is bold, almost rambunctious, with humor springing from exaggerated situations and jolting surprises.

COUNTEE CULLEN (1903-1946) was born in New York City, graduated from New York University and received his M.A. from Harvard University. He then became a teacher in New York City. His first book of poetry, *Color* (1925), brought him recognition as a leading Black American poet.

E. E. CUMMINGS (1894-1962) is widely known for his innovative approach to poetry—omitting punctuation and capitalization at will, slashing lines and even words to create a particular effect, and using excess word spacing as an accent in the rhythm. Many of his poetic experiments have been taken up by poets writing forty years after Cummings began. Mr. Cummings was born in Cambridge, Massachusetts, received his M.A. from Harvard University in 1916, and served with the Ambulance Corps during World War I. After the war he lived in Paris, gaining recognition as a painter as well as a writer. Later he returned to the United States and continued his experimentation with the arts.

DAVID DAICHES (1912-   ) was born in Sunderland, England, and lives in Sussex. After graduating from Edinburgh University and receiving his Ph.D. from Cambridge, he began teaching at Oxford University. Since then he has taught at the University of Chicago, Cornell University, Cambridge University, and the University of Sussex. He has written many books of literary criticism, literary biography, and literary history. His poetry, sketches, and short stories have appeared in *The New Yorker* and other magazines in the United States and England.

LEASA DAVIS (1956-   ) was born in Atlanta, Georgia, and currently is a student at Colgate University in Hamilton, New York. She has had several poems published in the high school magazine of Decatur, Georgia, Salem College literary magazine and *English Journal*. Among her hobbies are "playing my bassoon, back-packing, and stalking the wilds."

ANNIE DILLARD (1945-   ) grew up in Pittsburgh, Pa., attended Hollins College, and has lived in the Roanoke Valley of Virginia since 1965. *Pilgrim at Tinker Creek*, her first book, was hailed as "a book of wonder," recreating in flashing words the cycles of the seasons and the mystery of living things—ancient sycamores, starlings, muskrats, praying mantises, frogs. *Tickets for a Prayer Wheel* (1974) was her first book of poetry. Miss Dillard is a contributing editor of *Harper's* and a columnist for *The Living Wilderness*.

LAWRENCE FERLINGHETTI (1919 or 1920-   ) was born in Yonkers, New York, or Paris, his birth certificate being somewhat confused. He received his B.A. from the University of North Carolina, his master's degree from Columbia University, and from the Sorbonne, the *Doctorat de l'Université*. After World War II, he worked briefly for *Time*. He then became the founder and editor of City Lights Booksellers and Publishers of San Francisco. Lawrence Ferlinghetti believes strongly that poetry is to be read aloud. He composes much of his poetry on the tape recorder and has had great success in reading to large audiences. His books of poetry include *Pictures of a Gone World* (1955), *A Coney Island of the Mind* (1958), and *Starting from San Francisco* (1951). He has also published two plays and a novel, and has made numerous recordings of poetry readings.

KATHLEEN FRASER (1937-   ) was educated at Occidental College in Los Angeles. Her first book of poetry, *Change of Address*, was published in 1966. A collection of poems for children is entitled *Stilts, Somersalts and Headstands: Game Poems Based on a Painting by Peter Breughel* (1968). Kathleen Fraser lives in San Francisco.

NIKKI GIOVANNI (1943-   ) was born in Knoxville, Tennessee, and grew up in Cincinnati. She has been writing poetry ever since she was a child and has become one of the important new Black poets. Her books of poetry include *Black Feeling, Black Talk* (1968), *Re:Creation* (1970), *My House* (1972), and for children: *Spin a Soft Black Song* (1971), and *Ego-Tripping* (1973).

THERESA GREENWOOD was born in Cairo, Illinois, and has lived in the Middle West most of her life. She graduated from Millikin University and received her master's degree and her doctorate from Ball State University. Her poetry has appeared in several magazines, including *Saturday Evening Post* and *English Journal*. *Psalms of a Black Mother*, her first book of poetry, was published in 1970. Mrs. Greenwood, a teacher of elementary students, lives in Muncie, Indiana, with her husband (an assistant professor at Ball State) and their two young children.

TERRI HAAG was a senior in 1971 at Sunnyside High School in Tucson, Arizona, when her poem "Truck Drivers" won a prize in the Scholastic Creative Writing Awards competition.

GERALD HAUSMAN (1945-   ) was born in Baltimore, Maryland, and graduated from New Mexico Highlands University in Las Vegas, New Mexico. Currently he lives in Monterey, Massachusetts, where he works as a free-lance editor and writer. His poetry has appeared in a number of magazines, including *Sage* and *Desert Review*. His published books are *Circle Meadow, New Marlboro Stage,* and *Sitting on the Blue-Eyed Bear.*

ROBERT HAYDEN (1913-   ) was born in Detroit, Michigan, and attended Wayne State University and the University of Michigan. He has received fellowships from the Rosenwald and Ford Foundations and has been teaching at Fisk University since 1946. His poetry has won numerous awards, including the Grand Prize at the First World Festival of the Arts (Dakkar, 1966) for A *Ballad of Remembrance.*

CALVIN C. HERNTON (1933-   ) was born in Chattanooga, Tennessee, and was educated at Fisk University and Talladega College. His poetry has appeared in a number of magazines in this country and abroad. He is also the author of a collection of poetry, *The Coming of Chronos to the House of Nightsong* (1963). As a sociologist he has written several significant books including *Sex and Racism in America* (1965), and *White Paper for White Americans* (1966). Mr. Hernton teaches at Oberlin College in Ohio.

SANDRA HOCHMAN (1936-   ) was born in New York City and makes her home there today. After graduating from Bennington College in Vermont, she studied at the Sorbonne in Paris. Back in New York she became an actress, appearing in a number of off-Broadway productions. She has had several volumes of poetry published and frequently gives poetry readings.

PATRICIA HUBBELL (1928-   ) has lived most of her life in and around Easton and Westport, Connecticut. As an enthusiastic horseback rider, she has explored the Connecticut countryside and admits that many of her poems begin to emerge while she is riding. She has written three books of poetry for children: *The Apple Vendor's Fair* (1963); *8 A.M. Shadows* (1965); and *Catch Me a Wind* (1968). Her poems show amazing variety—ranging in theme from fairies and pheasants to bulldozers and the washing machine.

LANGSTON HUGHES (1902-1967) was working as a bus boy in a Washington hotel when he was discovered by Vachel Lindsay. His first volume of poetry, *The Weary Blues*, was published in 1926. At about the same time, a number of Black poets were breaking into print, all part of the Harlem Renaissance. Their poetry echoed the sounds of Black conversation and the rhythm of Black music, both spirituals and jazz. Many of these poets expressed despair over the plight of the Negro, but it was well-controlled despair, often alternating with laughter. Later poems by Langston Hughes, in *The Panther and the Lash* (1967), for example, express mounting anger over racial injustice but never with the violent protest of the younger Black poets of the late sixties and early seventies. Hughes was born in Joplin, Missouri, traveled widely, and then settled in Harlem. His published work—in addition to poetry—includes song lyrics, essays, short stories, plays, an autobiography, and several anthologies.

DAVID IGNATOW [*Ig-náy-tow*] (1914-   ) was born in Brooklyn and has lived most of his life in metropolitan New York. As teacher or poet in residence, he has been associated with Columbia University, Long Island University, Vassar College, and the universities of Kansas and Kentucky. For ten years he was editor of the *Beloit Poetry Journal*, then poetry editor of *The Nation*, and currently is co-editor of *Chelsea*. He has had four books of poetry published, the most recent being *David Ignatow: Poems 1934-1969*.

BROOKS JENKINS was a student at the New Hampton School for Boys in New Hampton, N.H., when he won an award for the poem "Loneliness." In the same year, 1935, he won a prize in Scholastic's Creative Writing Awards competition for the same poem.

LE ROI JONES. *See* Imamu Amiri Baraka

ERICA JONG (-   ) is probably best known for her novel, *Fear of Flying* (1973), which became a runaway best seller in both hardcover and paperback. Her first book, a collection of poetry entitled, *Fruits & Vegetables* (1971), brought her immediate recognition as a poet of unabashed candor whose work is sometimes playful, sometimes grave. Two subsequent volumes of poetry and many poems in magazines and anthologies have given Erica Jong a wide audience.

NORMAN JORDAN (1938-   ) was born in Ansted, West Virginia. Although he dropped out of junior high school, he has become a well known playwright and poet. He works with the students of the Muntu Workshop of Cleveland. Jordan has had two plays produced and two volumes of poetry published. His poems have appeared in many of the little magazines as well as in such anthologies as *The New Black Poetry* (1969), *Black Out Loud* (1970), and *Black Spirits* (1972).

JAMES JOYCE (1941-   ) was born in Oakland, California, and received his master's degree from San Francisco State University. Currently he is a teacher of computer sciences at the University of California at Berkeley. His publications include a number of articles on the use of computers in the study and analysis of literature and literary forms. When he was an eighth grader, his English teacher required each student to write a poem. "It was agony to write," he says now. "I continued to write poems—and they're still agony to write."

GALWAY KINNELL (1927-   ) was born in Providence, Rhode Island. In 1948 he received his B.A. from Princeton University and a year later his master's degree from the University of Rochester. He was a Fullbright Fellow in Paris in 1955-56, has taught in Grenoble, France, and the University of Tehran, Iran. In 1961 he received a Guggenheim Fellowship and an award from the National Institute of Arts and Letters. At several universities in the United States he has been designated Poet in Residence. In his early poetry he used traditional meter. More recently, inspired by Whitman and the poetry of William Carlos Williams, he has used free verse. His books of poetry: *What a Kingdom It Was* (1960), *Flower Herding on Mount Monadnock* (1964), *Poems of Night* (1968), *Body Rags* (1968). Mr. Kinnell lives in Sheffield, Vermont.

GARY KIZER (1946-   ) was born in Salamanca, New York. He reports that he began writing poetry "in response to the isolation and silence in Unit 14, Clinton Prison, 1970." While completing two years of college in the University Without Walls at Comstock, New York, he has had a number of poems published in small magazines. Currently he is working on a series of documentary poems which follow the transition of a single family from the rural south to the industrial north in the past 40 years.

STANLEY KUNITZ (1905-   ) was born in Worcester, Massachusetts, and graduated from Harvard University. For a number of years he taught at Bennington College and then at the State University of New York at Potsdam. Later he came to New York City where he became director of the poetry workshop at the YMHA and taught at Columbia University. His poetry has appeared in many anthologies and magazines. In 1959 he won the Pulitzer Prize for his *Selected Poems*.

MADELEINE L'ENGLE (1918-   ) was born in New York City. After graduating from Smith College, she returned to New York to work in the theater, playing several productions with Eva LeGallienne. After her marriage to Hugh Franklin, who was also acting in the Eva LeGallienne troupe, Madeleine L'Engle turned to writing. She is best known for her fiction for young adults. *A Wrinkle in Time*, a story about galactic space, won the Newbery Medal in 1962, an especially welcome honor because the manuscript had been turned down by 20 or more publishers before one agreed to bring it out. Her one book of poetry, *Lines Scribbled on an Envelope*, was published in 1969. The Franklins live in New York City, but spend their summers in an old farmhouse in the foothills of the Berkshires.

DENISE LEVERTOV (1923-   ) was born in England and served as a nurse during World War II. Her first book, *The Double Image*, was published in England in 1946. She married an American, Mitchell Goodman, and has been living in the United States since 1948. She has held a Guggenheim Fellowship and has served as poetry editor of *The Nation*. Her poems have been published in many periodicals. Her books include *Here and Now* (1957), *With Eyes at the Back of Our Heads* (1960), *The Jacob's Ladder* (1961), *O Taste and See* (1964), *The Sorrow Dance* (1967), *Relearning the Alphabet* (1970), *To Stay Alive* (1971), and *Footprints* (1972).

MYRA COHN LIVINGSTON (1926-   ) was born in Omaha, Nebraska, and enjoyed what she calls "an ideal childhood." From an early age, she has been interested in writing and in music. When she was eleven, her family moved to Los Angeles, where she wrote for her high school newspaper, studied the French horn, and played with the California Junior Symphony. After graduating from Sarah Lawrence College, she returned to California to write for Los Angeles newspapers and do public relations for Hollywood personalities.

Her first book of poetry for children was *Whispers and Other Poems* (Harcourt 1958). Since then, twelve collections of her poems and five anthologies have been published. Mrs. Livingston and her husband live in Beverly Hills, California.

JOHN LOGAN (1923-   ) was born in Red Oak, Iowa. He received his bachelor's degree from Coe College and his M.A. from the University of Iowa. Since 1966 he has been professor of English at the State University of New York in Buffalo. He has had several collections of poetry published as well as one play and several volumes of literary criticism.

PHYLLIS McGINLEY (1905-   ) was born in Oregon, but her family soon moved to Colorado where she lived until she was 12. She graduated from the University of Utah, studied at the University of California, and has since received honorary degrees from nine colleges and universities. At the age of six she began writing poetry, and by the time she was in college, her poems were appearing in leading national magazines. In 1961 she won the Pulitzer Prize for Poetry for her collection of verse entitled *Times Three*. She is the author of the best-seller, *Sixpence in Her Shoe* (1964), ten volumes of poetry, and more than a dozen children's books, including such favorites as *The Horse Who Lived Upstairs* (1944), *The Year Without a Santa Claus* (1957), *Boys Are Awful* (1962), and *A Wreath of Christmas Legends* (1967). The poet and her husband, Charles L. Hayden, live in Larchmont, N. Y.

GORDON MASSMAN (1949-   ) was born in Corpus Christi, Texas, received his B.S. from the University of Texas and his M.F.A. from the University of Alaska in Anchorage. Currently he is a representative of the New York publisher, W. W. Norton Inc., as traveler and field editor. His poems have been published in *Southern Poetry Review*, *Northwest Review*, *Texas Quarterly*, and *West Coast Poetry Review*. Mr. Massman, his wife and infant daughter live in Austin, Texas.

EDGAR LEE MASTERS (1869-1950) is best known for his *Spoon River Anthology* (1915), a collection of poetic monologues by 244 former inhabitants (both real and imagined) of Spoon River, near Lewiston and Petersburg, Illinois. All are dead and speak from their graves in a Midwestern cemetery. Although Masters turned out books at the rate of nearly one a year—poetry, plays, biographies, essays and one novel—none approached *Spoon River*. He was born in Garnett, Kansas. In 1895 he moved to Chicago where he practiced law for nearly 30 years.

WILLIAM H. MATCHETT (1923-   ) was born in Chicago. As a Quaker he became a conscientious objector during World War II. Later he graduated from Swarthmore College and received his doctorate from Harvard University. He began writing poetry as a student at the Westtown School in Pennsylvania. His first book of poetry, *Water Ouzel and Other Poems*, was published in 1954. Dr. Matchett is professor of English at the University of Washington in Seattle.

EVE MERRIAM (1916-   ) is a rarity among the poets writing for children because of her sharp commentary on the fancies and foibles of our plastic world. Appropriately, her verse forms are innovative. Her subject matter is all-encompassing; her moods are kaleidoscopic—gay, satiric, blunt, teasing, gentle, but never static. She was born in Philadelphia and graduated from the University of Pennsylvania. She has taught creative writing at City College of New York and the Bank Street College of Education. Her poetry for adults and for children shows wide-ranging interests and diversity of style. Eve Merriam and her husband, Leonard C. Lewin, also a writer, divide their time between their Riverside Drive apartment in New York and their house in Stonington, Connecticut.

EDNA ST. VINCENT MILLAY (1892-1950) was born in Maine, graduated from Vassar College, and came to New York for a literary career. Her first published volume, *Renascence* (1917), took its title from a long poem written when Miss Millay was scarcely 19. Her poems show her relentless concern with beauty and youth's romantic and rebellious spirit. *Poems Selected for Young People* (1951) reflects the deeply personal, vibrant quality to which many of today's young readers are attuned.

BILL MESSENGER (1937-   ) was born William Moessinger on Long Island, New York. He holds a master of arts degree and has been enrolled in Johns Hopkins University Writing Seminars. Currently he is a sheep farmer and writes a weekly column for the Baltimore Sunday *News American* about life on the farm. His hobbies include foraging for wild foods, collecting marine mollusks, and working as a professional jazz pianist. His poetry writing grew out of his work as a composer of popular songs. Mr. Moessinger lives on Little Brook Farm near Street, Maryland.

LISEL MUELLER was born in Germany and came to the United States as a teenager. She is a graduate of Evansville College and has studied also at Indiana University. *Dependencies*, her first book of poetry, was published in 1965. She lives near Chicago with her husband and two children.

LEONARD NATHAN (1924-   ), a native of Los Angeles, received his Ph.D. from the University of California at Berkeley, where he has been a professor of speech for a number of years. He has had over 200 poems published in more than 35 literary journals and national magazines.

KENNETH PATCHEN (1911-   ) was born in Ohio and attended the University of Wisconsin. Although bedridden as the result of a childhood injury to his back, he has written numerous books of poetry, has recorded poetry readings, and often illustrates his own work in handmade limited editions. In 1967 the National Endowment for the Arts recognized "his lifelong contribution to American letters." His books include *When We Were Here Together* (1957), *Because It Is*

(1960), *Sleepers Awake* (1969), and *Aflame and Afun of Walking Faces* (1970). He and his wife live in Palo Alto, California.

MARGE PIERCY (1936-   ) was born in Detroit. Her poems have appeared in *The Carleton Miscellany, The Transatlantic Review,* and other magazines. She has had two novels published as well as several books of poetry including *Breaking Camp* (1968) and *Hard Loving* (1969). She lives in Wellfleet, Massachusetts.

FELIX POLLACK (1909-   ) was born in Vienna. He became a lawyer in Austria and also studied to be a stage director. When he moved to the United States, he became a librarian and now serves as curator of rare books at the University of Wisconsin in Madison. He has had several collections of poetry published. In addition, his poems have been included in anthologies and in small magazines of the United States, Germany, and Austria.

NANCY REMALY (1959-   ) was born in Carlisle, Pennsylvania, where she is now a high school student. Her poems have appeared in her school literary paper and *English Journal.* As a high school sophomore she won first and second place in the Cumberland County Poetry Contest. As a high school junior she won a scholarship to the Pennsylvania Governor's School for the Arts where she studied creative writing.

CHARLES REZNIKOFF (1894-   ) was born in Brooklyn, studied journalism at the University of Missouri, and graduated from the Law School of New York University. He has had numerous books of poetry published including *By the Waters of Manhattan* (1962) and *By the Well of Living and Seeing* (1973). His poetry is simple and terse, focusing on such familiar scenes and people as the derelicts of New York city streets and the scrubwomen in dank hallways. According to one critic, "He is a deep, sarcastic, lonely writer."

BARBARA B. ROBINSON (1921-   ) was born in Honolulu and has her master's degree from the University of Hawaii. When she began teaching in 1962, she tested her assignments for her students by doing them herself. As she puts it: "I'm learning to write along with

158

my students." She has had several stories and poems published in local and national magazines. Two books of poetry are under way—one about the Island of Oahu and the other a how-to book of concrete poetry. Barbara Robinson lives in Honolulu on the Island of Oahu.

THEODORE ROETHKE [Ret'-kee] (1908-1963) was born in Saginaw, Michigan, where he lived until he entered the University of Michigan. He did graduate work at Harvard University and then taught English in several colleges and universities in the East before moving to Seattle, where he taught at the University of Washington until his death.

In 1941 his first book of poetry, *Open House*, was published. Subsequent collections of poetry won for him numerous honors and awards: the Pulitzer Prize, the Bollingen Prize, two National Book Awards, and two Guggenheim Fellowships. Two poetry collections are especially for children: *I Am! Says the Lamb* (1961) and *Dirty Dinkie and Other Poems* (1973).

CARL SANDBURG (1878-1967) was born in Galesburg, Illinois, the son of Swedish immigrants. He left school at 13 and began driving a milk wagon. Then followed a succession of jobs: working in a barber shop, scene-shifting in a cheap theater, railroad building in the far west, dishwashing in Denver and Omaha, pitching wheat in Kansas, fighting in Puerto Rico in the Spanish-American War, working his way through college, and then a period of newspaper work. When Sandburg was 36, his first poems were published in *Poetry Magazine*. A year later came the publication of his first book of poetry, *Chicago Poems* (1916), which produced a storm of debate. Critics called it brutal, unpoetic, colloquial, ugly, distorted. His defenders noted the poetic metaphors in his use of slang, the tenderness in his toughness. Thirty-four years and many books later, Carl Sandburg won the Pulitzer Prize for his *Complete Poems* (1950). His six-volume life of Abraham Lincoln is considered one of the great American biographies. One of his most intriguing books is *The American Songbag*, a collection of 280 folk songs, with music, which he gathered from mountain people, work gangs, cowboys, and hoboes.

In his sixties Carl Sandburg and his wife moved from the Middle West, where they had spent most of their lives, to a 240-acre farm in the Great Smokies of North Carolina.

ANNE SEXTON (1928-1974) was born in Newton, Massachusetts. Her first book of poetry, *To Bedlam and Part Way Back* (1960), is poignant, sometimes painful, as the poet speaks sharply of her sense of guilt and mental torment. In 1966 she won the Pulitzer Prize for her third book of poetry, *Live or Die*. Her poems have appeared in such magazines as *Harper's*, *Hudson Review*, and *The New Yorker*. In the fall of 1974 Anne Sexton committed suicide two days after giving a sparkling reading of her poetry to a cheering audience of college students.

SHEL SILVERSTEIN was born in Chicago, grew up in the midwest, and today is an inveterate cross-country traveler. He is famous for his drawings which appear regularly in *Playboy* magazine. In the world of country folk music, he is well known for his lyrics, including the hit song "A Boy Named Sue." He has written and illustrated several highly original books: *Lafcadio, the Lion Who Shot Back*, *The Giving Tree*, and *Where the Sidewalk Ends*, a collection of poems and drawings.

GARY SNYDER (1930-   ) was born in San Francisco, graduated from Reed College, and studied at Indiana University and the University of California at Berkeley. He studied Buddhism in Japan during the years 1956-64. He lists his occupational skills as "logging, forestry, carpentry, seaman." Gary Snyder has been the recipient of several awards, prizes, grants and fellowships. He has published a book of essays and nine volumes of poetry, including *Riprap and Cold Mountain* (1959) and *Myths and Texts* (1960).

ALBERT SPECTOR (1921-   ) was born in Boston and received his B.A. and M.A. from The City College of New York. He is a high school English teacher on Long Island. He has had articles published in *English Journal* and the *Long Island Press*.

WILLIAM STAFFORD (1914-   ) was born in Hutchinson, Kansas, of Indian ancestry. He received his B.A. and M.A. from the University of Kansas and his doctorate from the State University of Iowa. During World War II, he was a conscientious objector, his alternate work being with the Forest Service. Since 1948 he has taught English literature and composition at Lewis and Clark College in Portland,

Oregon. In 1962, his second book of poetry, *Traveling through the Dark*, received the National Book Award with the citation "William Stafford's poems are clean, direct and whole. They are both tough and gentle; their music knows the value of silence." He has also received the Shelley Memorial Award of the Poetry Society of America and a Guggenheim Foundation Award, and has served as poetry consultant to the Library of Congress. Mr. Stafford, whose poems have been widely anthologized, lives in Lake Oswego, Oregon, with his wife and their four children. All are campers, bicyclers, travelers, and readers.

ADRIEN STOUTENBURG (1913-   ) was born in Minnesota, has traveled extensively in Mexico, Holland, and the British Isles, and now lives in California. She received the Edwin Markham Award from the Poetry Society of America (1961) and the Lamont Poetry Award of the American Academy of Poets in 1964. Her poems have appeared in *The New Yorker, The Nation* and numerous poetry magazines. History and nature—particularly wild animals—have a predominant place in her work. Her books include *American Tall Tales* (1968), *Vanishing Thunder: Extinct and Threatened Bird Species* (1967), *The Crocodile's Mouth: Folk-Song Stories* (1966) and, with Laura N. Baker, *Listen America: A Life of Walt Whitman* (1968).

MIKE TODACHINE, a Navajo Indian, was a teenager when he wrote the poem beginning "you can look into my face/ and all you see is a very old face." It was included in *Song of the Earth Spirit* published by Friends of the Earth in 1973.

MARGARET TSUDA was born in New York and attended Hunter College, where she was a fine arts major. Her articles on the fine arts have appeared in *The Christian Science Monitor* and *The New Jersey Music and Arts Magazine*. "The need for a more precise communication than painting or drawing allows" directed her to writing poetry. Two volumes of her poetry have been published: *Cry Love Aloud* (1972) and *Urban River* (1976). Mrs. Tsuda lives in Newark, N.J.

JOHN UPDIKE (1932-   ), winner of numerous awards for his novels, poetry, and short stories for adults, was born in Shillington, Pennsylvania, graduated from Harvard University and studied at Oxford. For two years he was on the editorial staff of *The New Yorker*, which has published many of his stories. His first book of poetry, *The Carpentered Hen and Other Strange Creatures* (1958), has been followed by several collections, including *A Child's Calendar* (1965) for children. For his fiction he has won the Rosenthal Award (1960), the National Book Award (1964) and the O. Henry Award (1966). Mr. Updike, his wife and two children live in Ipswich, Massachusetts.

MARK VAN DOREN (1894-1972) was born in Hope, Illinois. He received his Ph.D. from Columbia University and was a professor of English there for 39 years. During a long and distinguished literary career he edited several anthologies of poetry, letters, and biographies and had many books of his own original work published—poetry, drama, fiction, non-fiction, and four children's books. Sixteen volumes of his poetry were published, his *Collected Poems* winning the Pulitzer Prize in 1939.

TOM WEBER, a native of New York's Hell's Kitchen, has been a photo-journalist since he was 18 years old. He has been a stevedore on the San Francisco waterfront and a commercial fisherman. He has worked as a reporter, editor, and photographer on metropolitan newspapers and magazines, including *The San Francisco Chronicle* and *The Peninsula Herald* of Monterey, California. Weber has been around the world four times, taking photographs of people in every major nation of the world. He lives in Monterey with his wife and family.

WALT WHITMAN (1819-1892) was born on Long Island, New York, and grew up in Brooklyn. As a 12-year-old he learned the skills of a printer. Later he worked as a journalist on several newspapers, including the *Brooklyn Eagle* and *New Orleans Crescent*. In 1848 he began writing poetry, but he found no publisher who would accept his innovative style. Finally he published 12 poems at his own expense under the title *Leaves of Grass* (1855). For the rest of his life he kept adding to this collection, which was either ignored or ridiculed by most of the critics. During the Civil War, he worked as a volunteer assistant in a military hospital in Washington, D.C. Today, *Leaves of Grass* is considered one of the world's major literary works.

SIV WIDERBERG (her first name rhymes with "weave") is a Swedish author who has written many poems, stories, and plays for children.

She is also the editor of the children's news page of a large Stockholm daily newspaper. Her collection of poems for children, *I'm Like Me,* was translated from the Swedish by Verne Moberg and published in the United States by Feminist Press.

TENNESSEE WILLIAMS (1914-   ) is best known as a playwright, having twice won the Pulitzer Prize for Drama (*A Streetcar Named Desire,* 1948, and *Cat on a Hot Tin Roof,* 1955). *The Glass Menagerie* won the Drama Critics Award in 1945. Several of his plays have been the basis for widely distributed movies and have been adapted into television dramas. In addition, he has had two collections of poetry published (1944 and 1956). Williams was born in Columbus, Mississippi, graduated from the University of Iowa, and now divides his time between New York City and Key West, Florida.

WILLIAM CARLOS WILLIAMS (1883-1963) was highly successful in two careers which he carried on simultaneously. For more than 40 years he was a practicing pediatrician in his home town of Rutherford, N.J. When only 21, his first book of poetry was published. He continued to write and receive literary awards throughout his life. His *Pictures from Breughel* won the 1963 Pulitzer Prize for poetry. Williams's poetic lines are full of conversational speech and, wrote Louis Untermeyer, "express the brusque nervous tension, the vigor and the rhetoric of American life." In addition to books of poetry, his publications include a book of essays and one of plays.

JAMES WRIGHT (1927-   ) was born in Martins Ferry, Ohio, and grew up there. He graduated from Kenyon College, later receiving his Ph.D. from the University of Washington in Seattle. Since 1966 he has been professor of English at Hunter College in New York City. He has had three books of poetry published and has translated the work of a number of German and Spanish poets as well. His poetry has won several awards, including the Robert Frost Prize.

INDEX OF FIRST LINES